D1128437

GUTSY JOBS

Diane Lindsey Reeves

Ferguson

An imprint of Infobase Publishing

Acknowledgements

Special thanks to Sam Carothers, Lonnie Knudsen, Mike Odle, and Nguyen Xuan Phong for sharing their stories about their distinctly different and daring work. Thanks also to Joy Strickland, Catherine Davis, and Lacey Reeves, who assisted in researching and writing this book.

Way Out Work: Gutsy Jobs

Copyright © 2009 by Diane Lindsey Reeves

Ferguson
An imprint of Infobase Publishing
132 West 31st Street
New York, NY 10001

Library of Congress Cataloging-in-Publication Data
Reeves, Diane Lindsey, 1959–
   Gutsy jobs / Diane Lindsey Reeves.
      p. cm.—(Way out work)
   Includes index.
   ISBN-13: 978-1-60413-133-8 (hbk. : alk. paper)
   ISBN-10: 1-60413-133-0 (hbk. : alk. paper)   1. Job descriptions—Juvenile literature. 2. Occupations—Juvenile literature. 3. Vocational guidance—Juvenile literature. I. Title.
   HF5381.2.R444 2009
   331.702—dc22

                              2009008228

Ferguson books are available at special discounts when purchased in bulk quantities for businesses, associations, institutions, or sales promotions. Please call our Special Sales Department in New York at (212) 967-8800 or (800) 322-8755.

You can find Ferguson on the World Wide Web at http://www.fergpubco.com

Text design by Erika K. Arroyo
Cover design by Jooyoung An

Printed in the United States of America

Bang MSRF 10 9 8 7 6 5 4 3 2 1

This book is printed on acid-free paper.

Contents

Introduction

Have you ever wished you could be a superhero? You just might be in luck. People find tons of ways to make heroic acts a regular part of their work—minus the tights and capes, of course. In fact, many people do things every day that most people would never have the guts to do even once.

These gutsy people routinely do things like fight fires, investigate airplane and automobile crashes, negotiate international peace treaties, help ease very sick people through their last days, and confront dangerous criminals. Some are even brave enough to face rooms full of rambunctious kids in school classrooms around the world!

What do they do and how do they do it? And, perhaps most puzzling of all, why do some people willingly put themselves on the line (and even in great danger) just to help others? Stay tuned for answers to these questions and more as you read about jobs that require equal amounts of courage and skill.

Here's where you'll find profiles introducing several heroic jobs and encounter interesting features sure to get you thinking in new and unexpected ways. Then take a quick look at more gutsy job ideas, and stop by to read about people who are doing some rather courageous work. Spend a little time at the end of the book where you can do some activities to find out once and for all if you've got what it takes to do a gutsy job.

Crash Scene Investigator

An air crash investigator looks at the engine of a crashed aircraft. *Rui Vieira/PA Photos/Landov*

Planes, trains, boats, automobiles, and even space shuttles. . . They get people where they want to go. Most of the time. Sometimes, though, the worst happens and an accident stops some of these vehicles in their tracks—often with great damage to occupants and property alike.

What went wrong and how did it happen? Those are key questions that investigators tackle when they are called to a crash site. They gather evidence, interview witnesses, and take photographs to get a sense of the chain of events. They measure the area using lasers to create a digital map of the scene and they look for any possible clues as to the cause of the crash. They inspect the involved vehicles for damage, determine the point of impact, and, when necessary, figure out if human error or a mechanical malfunction is to blame.

In cases of especially complicated accidents, they may later recreate accident scenes to see for themselves how things went so badly awry. This process, at times, can be easier said than done. It involves careful imitation of the situation, the speed, and

Gutsy Factor

Making the world safer to go.

even the weather conditions to find out the chain of events.

While investigating automobile accidents is tricky enough, can you imagine what it might be like to investigate an airplane crash? In these situations (which, thankfully are extremely rare), investigators could be dealing with multiple victims as well as staggering amounts of data and debris. Many times the investigation involves painstakingly gathering every piece of wreckage and reassembling it in an airport hangar. That way, months or even years later, investigators may be able to pinpoint the exact cause of the crash.

What Do You Think?
According to the Centers for Disease Control and Prevention, child safety seats reduce the risk of death in passenger cars by 71 percent for infants and by 54 percent for toddlers ages 1 to 4. Given that car seats are so effective, why would any parent not use them? What are some ways to encourage all parents to use them?

WOW!

Did you know that the first automobile was created in 1769? It was propelled by steam instead of gas, and it was supposed to be used by the French army. It wasn't very popular, though—it only went 2.5 miles an hour!

GO FOR IT IF. . .

You're good at
solving mysteries.

- - - - - - - - - - - - - - -

You can't imagine yourself that
close to gory crash scenes.

FORGET ABOUT IT IF. . .

Once all the evidence has been gathered and the crash site cleared, investigators' work kicks into high gear. They return to their offices and work with other experts to process and analyze all of the evidence. This can be rather routine in simple "fender bender" cases. But in those with significant injuries, loss of life, or massive damage, every piece of evidence must be documented and explained. The investigator's conclusions are often used as evidence in court cases where negligent drivers or companies might be sued or prosecuted for possible crimes. Insurance companies also use the investigator's reports to reach settlement agreements with the people affected by the accident.

One of the most important results of an investigator's work occurs when they discover something that can prevent other accidents. This might involve fixing a mechanical defect in certain kinds of vehicles, improving road conditions with repairs or road signs, or even learning something new from an unfortunate mistake.

**Go Online
to Find Out More!**
Re-create a crash scene like the ones real investigators face at http://www. edheads.org/activities/ crash_scene.

Diplomat

Foreign diplomats meet to discuss relations among their respective countries. *Airedale Brothers/Getty Images*

Have you ever had a disagreement with a sibling or a friend that got so hot that a teacher or parent had to step in to help sort things out? You both had very specific ideas about the way you wanted things to be and neither one of you was willing to give in. If you were lucky, the adult helped you look at the situation through the other person's eyes so that you could reach a fair compromise that worked for both of you.

Sound familiar? If so, you have experienced on a personal level what a diplomat does. The biggest difference is that instead of mediat-

Being a peacemaker.

ing disagreements between a couple of stubborn kids, diplomats do it for entire nations.

Diplomats act as representatives of their home country's government in other places around the world. Sometimes that means they travel to various places to conduct meetings or attend world summits. Other times that means they actually live in another country and work in an embassy. In many cases, diplomats specialize in a certain part of the world—learning the language and culture, studying the history, and cultivating an understanding of the country's important issues.

Although the specifics of different kinds of diplomatic job responsibilities differ greatly, all diplomats share the common purpose of building a bridge of friendship between the two governments. Sometimes this means helping a U.S. citizen who encounters difficulties while traveling in a foreign country. Other times it means providing aid to a country after a natural disaster. At its highest levels, diplomacy involves brokering peace on earth.

What Do You Think?

If you could become a diplomat any place in the world, which country would you pick? Why?

WOW!

Diplomats need to master at least one other language. Deciding which one to learn can be a challenge since there are currently 6,912 languages spoken in various places around the world.

GO FOR IT IF . . .

You'd love to see the world.

– – – – – – – – – – – – – – –

You get homesick just going across the street to visit a friend.

FORGET ABOUT IT IF . . .

In the United States, most diplomatic work comes under the domain of the Department of State, which is headed by the secretary of state. This person is appointed by the president (and approved by Congress) to represent the country's interests abroad. The State Department hires, trains, and oversees the work of a diplomatic corps that circles the globe. The president also appoints ambassadors to lead embassies around the world. This is a very prestigious diplomatic position.

Most diplomats land their jobs through more conventional means than a presidential appointment. They get the education, gain the experience, and go through a rigorous interview and training process to earn the right to represent their nation's interests. Those most likely to succeed in diplomacy can communicate effectively in more than one language, are extremely knowledgeable about current events and world issues, and love to travel.

Of course, diplomacy is a two-way street. Just as the United States assigns diplomats and runs embassies in other countries, other countries assign diplomats and run embassies in the U.S. These foreign embassies are located in places like Washington, D.C., New York City (near the United Nations), and other major cities.

Go Online to Find Out More!

All aboard the United Nations Cyberschoolbus to learn more about the world at http://www.un.org/Pubs/ CyberSchoolBus.

Environmental Engineer

An environmental engineer records the water quality in a wetlands in Fishers, Indiana. *AP Photo/Michael Conroy*

Have you ever been stuck in a traffic jam and realized just how many cars there are on the road? Or have you had to carry trash to the dumpster, only to look in and see it's overflowing with trash bags? Maybe you've been on a picnic with your family and noticed that junk had washed up on the shore of the lake, making it look icky and gross?

Well, it's no secret that there are a lot of people on this planet—and a lot of people means a lot of trash and pollution! Some people have dedicated their lives to finding ways to reduce pollution and minimize human impact on the environment. These people are called environmental engineers, and they use the power of science to find eco-friendly solutions to problems.

Did you realize that you could use the things you learn in science and math classes to save the world? That's what environmental engineers do. They start with a solid background in subjects like biology, chemistry, physics, and high levels of math. They go to college to learn all they can about engineering. College is where they learn the secrets behind building bridges and skyscrapers and all kinds of engineering marvels.

Engineers take all that knowledge and look at ways to apply it to environmental problems. Some look at ways to build environmentally friendly houses. Others explore new ways to create energy using wind, solar power, and alternative fuels. Others look at more efficient ways to use our water supplies and to eliminate pollution. There's definitely not a shortage of problems to solve!

Engineering jobs are as varied as the problems engineers work on. Some become researchers, looking for better ways to do things that

What Do You Think?

Each year, 14 billion pounds of trash is dumped into our oceans, endangering all kinds of sea creatures. Can you think of something better to do with all those dirty diapers, stinky old shoes, and plastic jugs?

WOW!

Did you know that for each can of garbage you put out at the curb, 70 more cans were filled by all the processes needed to make the products (or packages) you just threw away?

GO FOR IT IF...

You are a
recycling fanatic!

- - - - - - - - - - - - - - -

Science and math aren't
exactly your best subjects
in school.

FORGET ABOUT IT IF...

impact the environment. Others become designers and planners, creating new types of housing, work-

places, and even cities that make more sense. Some become professors and share their knowledge with future engineers. In fact, there are so many different types of opportunities that you are just as likely to find an environmental engineer at an urban building site as you are in a far-off rainforest!

Go Online
to Find Out More!
See what you can do to
save the environment at
http://www.epa.gov/kids.

First Responder

A brave firefighter climbs through raging torrents of fire to reach people trapped in a burning building. *AP Photo/Observer-Dispatch, Michael Doherty*

Forget the capes and masks! Today's superheroes are more likely to wear a neatly pressed uniform and carry a badge. These gutsy people come to the rescue when things go really bad. They are the first people on the scene when fires break out, when crimes are committed, when people get hurt, or when accidents happen. That's why people like police officers, firefighters, paramedics, and other emergency workers are known collectively as first responders.

Dial 911 and within minutes these highly trained professionals are on the way to help. Paramedics, also known as EMTs (Emergency Medi-

What Do You Think?
What would the world be like if no one had the courage to be a first responder?

cal Technicians), are people you'll be glad to see if you are ever injured in a car accident or involved in some other type of health-related emergency. They rush to the scene to provide immediate care and to transport injured people to the hospital for further treatment. Many times the situations they encounter are truly a matter of life or death. But they are highly trained to react calmly and skillfully to all kinds of health care problems—someone suffering a heart attack or stroke, a person who has been shot or stabbed, or many people who have been injured in a natural disaster. Due to the horrible lessons learned after the 9/11 ter-

rorist attacks, paramedics are also trained to respond to man-made disasters as well.

Firefighters are another type of first responder. These heroes are famous for running into burning buildings when everyone else is running out. The very nature of their work puts them in harm's way on a regular basis. Through constant training and a lot of teamwork, they learn how to battle blazes caused by all kinds of circumstances including house fires, forest fires, chemical fires, and explosions. Of course, given the choice, they would much rather be preventing fires than fighting them!

Police officers are yet another type of first responder. Although there may be times that you'd rather not encounter one, like when you are zooming down the highway exceeding the speed limit, if you ever find yourself in a dangerous situation,

WOW!

Can you guess the number one reason why people call 911? It's automobile accidents. Better buckle up!

GO FOR IT IF...

You aren't afraid of anything (or almost anything)!

- - - - - - - - - - - - - - -

You freak out about every little thing.

FORGET ABOUT IT IF...

a police officer is a welcome sight. Police officers are responsible for keeping people safe. Sometimes that might involve something relatively simple like directing traffic when a traffic light malfunctions. Other times it involves confronting armed crimi-

nals who are caught "red handed" doing something that is definitely against the law—like robbing a bank or kidnapping a child. In other situations, police officers might be called to the scene of an accident, a domestic dispute, or even a murder. Being ready for anything is just part of a day's work.

It's not every job that can claim saving lives as a routine task but first responders do it all the time. That very fact is what makes putting their lives on the line every day worth it.

Go Online to Find Out More!

Find out what to do when the worst happens at http://www.fema.gov/kids.

Hospice Worker

A hospice worker listens to a terminally ill woman's heartbeat. *Dana Neely/Getty Images*

Nobody wants to be sick. But when stuck in bed with the chicken pox or (achoo!) the flu, we all love having somebody take care of us! Who doesn't like a little tender, loving care?

Hospice workers make it their lives' work to provide that kind of TLC to people who are really, really sick.

They tend to care for people in the last phases of a terrible, incurable disease. They step in when there is nothing else that doctors or hospitals can do to help the person. In many cases, their patients only have months, or weeks, or even just days left to live. Many of their patients are in the last stage of some form of cancer, while others

17

have heart disease, Alzheimer's, or AIDS.

With diseases like these, people often reach a point where the only thing that others can do is tend to care-giving tasks that keep them as comfortable as possible. This can involve administering pain medications, providing a soothing environment, and helping the person maintain a sense of dignity by keeping them clean and fed.

The word "hospice" may sound like it comes from "hospital," but it doesn't. The word actually comes from the word "hospitality." Knowing this can help you better understand the nature of the work. Although hospice workers may work in a hospital, they are just as likely to provide care in a person's own home or in another comfortable setting. And, while the care they give certainly has medical aspects to it, it also contains generous amounts of compassion and friendship that are more often associated with hospitality than with hospitals.

Many times a hospice worker helps the patient's loved ones as much or more than he or she helps the patient. It can be very hard to watch someone you care about go through such a difficult situation. Hospice workers provide comfort and help loved ones find ways to deal with their grief.

What Do You Think?
Why do you think that, given the chance, most terminally ill patients would prefer to die at home than at a hospital?

WOW!

According to the Hospice Association of America, 80 percent of hospice patients are age 65 or older.

GO FOR IT IF...

You've got a soft spot
for people who are sick.

— — — — — — — — — — — — —

You don't do
"peace and quiet"
very well.

FORGET ABOUT IT IF...

Some hospice workers are doctors or nurses, while others are social workers that help find specific types of help for their patients.

Some provide spiritual care as ministers, rabbis, or imams, while others act as counselors and therapists. Hospice work is also performed by thousands—some say as many as 95,000—volunteers every year, a fact that suggests how very important this work is considered.

Go Online to Find Out More!

Hospice workers have to take care of themselves in order to take care of others. Learn some healthy tips at http://www.kidnetic.com.

Politician

President Barack Obama speaks during his inauguration as the 44th president of the United States of America on January 20, 2009. *Alex Wong/Getty Images*

people, by the people, for the people." He said this back in 1863, but no one before then or since has described democracy better.

As a democratic republic, the citizens of the United States govern themselves. Does that mean everyone gets to do whatever they want to do? No, it means that everyone gets a say. And, one of the most important ways that Americans get a say is by voting for the people who govern them. These elected officials, or politicians, may serve the people at a local, state, or national level. For instance, mayors are in charge of towns and cities,

Standing on a Civil War battlefield in Gettysburg, Pennsylvania, then President Abraham Lincoln described democracy as a government "of the

What Do You Think? The United States is governed as a democratic republic where every citizen is free to voice his or her opinion. Would the world be a better place if every country were run this way? Why or why not?

governors are in charge of states, and the president, of course, governs the whole country. As chief executive, the president in turn shares his or her power with the legislative branch and the judicial branch. The legislative branch is made up of 435 representatives and 100 senators—all of which are elected by their home states and all of whom are also politicians. The judicial branch is made up of nine Supreme Court justices who are not elected and are not politicians. They are appointed by the president and must be approved by Congress.

Now that we've had a little civics lesson, you may be wondering what it is that politicians actually do. When they do their jobs right, politicians represent the best interests of the people who elected them by passing legislation that helps and protects them. Politicians at all levels are entrusted with protecting our most precious assets—from the right to pursue life, liberty, and happiness to safeguarding our national security and preserving our democratic way of life.

Before politicians get a chance to do this important work, however, they must get elected. Getting elected isn't easy and involves a great deal of time, energy, money, and most of all—plenty of political savvy. This process works a lot like the process your school may use to elect its student government: Someone decides to run for office, they find a group of supporters to help them win, they make speeches, they put up posters, they

WOW!

Politicians come from all walks of life. For instance, Ronald Reagan got his start as an actor. He appeared in 53 films before becoming governor of California and later being elected as the United State's 40th president.

GO FOR IT IF. . .

You're a natural leader.
Or is it naturally bossy?

– – – – – – – – – – – – – –

You'd rather work behind
the scenes than in
the spotlight.

FORGET ABOUT IT IF. . .

make promises, and do anything else they can think of to get their "vote for me" message out to anyone who will listen. Of course, all this is done on a larger scale than the typical school election, but you get the general idea, don't you?

Surprisingly, there aren't a whole lot of rules governing who can become a politician. There are age limits. A person must be at least 35 years of age to become president of the United States, for instance. There are citizenship requirements. A person running for office in the United States must be a citizen, and in most local elections they must actually live in the area they hope to represent. Other than that, politicians come from all walks of life and can be of any gender, any religion, and any ethnic background. Some politicians are well educated and well to do; some come from professional backgrounds like law, medicine, or business; while others are simply ordinary citizens who think they can do a better job than the person currently holding the office.

Go Online to Find Out More!

Find out all you ever wanted to know about government and politics by clicking links found at http://bensguide.gpo.gov.

Religious Leader

A preacher raises his Bible as he gives his sermon. *Moodboard/Corbis*

Do you get up early on Sunday mornings, put on your nicest clothes, and head to church for Sunday school? Or do you go to a mosque or kneel, facing Mecca, and pray five times a day? Or perhaps you head to the synagogue on Saturdays and listen to your Rabbi read from the Torah?

If so, you are like the nearly 86 percent of the world's population who believe in one of the world's 4,300 different forms of religion. Religious leaders offer guidance and teachings for people who share their faiths. Even though the actual belief systems may differ, all spiritual leaders share the common duties of providing spiritual and moral guidance, leading services and ceremonies, and acting as role models for the people in their faith communities.

23

Though there are thousands of different religions, there are five major world religions widely recognized for the significant number of followers they attract and for the way they have impacted world history. These religions are Christianity, Islam, Hinduism, Buddhism, and Judaism. Each of these religions recognizes their respective leaders with a different title. In Christianity, the leader is often called a pastor, minister, or priest; Islamic leaders are called imams; Hindu religious leaders are also called priests; Buddhist spiritual guides are monks; and Jewish leaders are called rabbis.

Some religious leaders work in very small communities, working through a local church, temple, or mosque to serve the people around them. Others lead mosques or synagogues or churches that have thousands of members and are well known, or even famous, for their wisdom and ministry. Other types of religious leaders go out into the world to

What Do You Think?
Besides the five main religions, how many religions can you name? Remember, there are more than 4,300 of them!

WOW!

What is the world's oldest form of religion? It depends on whom you ask. Some would say Hinduism, while others would say Zoroastrianism. Both religions originated around 1500 BCE—that's about 1,500 years before Christianity, and more than 2,000 before Islam!

GO FOR IT IF...

You want to spend your life helping others.

- - - - - - - - - - - - - -

You can't see yourself spending that much time in a place of worship.

FORGET ABOUT IT IF...

work with people in other countries. These leaders are known as missionaries, and they travel into some of the most dangerous jungles and deserts and icy tundra to tell people about their beliefs. Other types of religious leaders organize and lead international relief efforts, taking food and medicine to people in need and providing help in times of trouble (such as the aftermath of a natural disaster). No matter the specifics of their individual faiths, most religious leaders try to live lives that encourage their followers to be good and do good.

Go Online to Find Out More!
Explore the world and its many religions at http://www. worldalmanacforkids.com

Social Worker

A social worker consults with a client. *Dave Dieter/The Huntsville Times/Landov*

Social workers are unsung heroes. You rarely read about them on the front page of newspapers. They generally don't get schools or roads named after them. Even though they often save people's lives, they don't attract the same level of attention as someone who pulls people out of burning buildings and does other courageous deeds of a more obvious nature.

Social workers focus on three main types of problems: family issues, health issues, and mental

What Do You Think?

How do you think social workers handle dealing with other people's problems all the time?

26

Gutsy Factor

Helping people with problems get a second chance.

health issues. And, in case you are wondering, there is no shortage of people needing help in any of these areas.

Social workers who focus on family issues work with children and parents in a wide variety of ways. This might involve investigating child abuse allegations and taking steps to protect children from harm. It might involve teaching new parents how to care for their baby, or it might involve helping those who want to become parents adopt a child. Some social workers help families who are going through a divorce, while others work with children in school settings—helping to identify and respond to different types of learning or behavioral problems. Others work with families who are having financial difficulties by helping to manage public assistance programs and training people for new opportunities.

Social workers who focus on public health issues help people get the medical care they need to get better. This can involve anything from helping someone find a good surgeon to helping patients with a particular disease learn to care for themselves. Social workers may work with people who have been victims of crimes or who suffered some kind of traumatic injury or situation. They may offer counseling and support to a person who has lost a loved one. Some work as health care advocates, standing up

WOW!

According to the Bureau of Labor Statistics, the need for social workers is expected to grow twice as fast as other occupations—especially in gerontology (elder care), home health care, substance abuse, private social service agencies, and school social work.

GO FOR IT IF...

You are the first person friends turn to when they are in trouble.

- - - - - - - - - - - - - -

You tend to find yourself in more trouble than you know what to do with.

FORGET ABOUT IT IF...

for patients to make sure that they get the care they need.

Other social workers focus on helping people with mental health and substance abuse problems. They provide counseling and therapy and make sure they get any medications they need to stay healthy. They help them learn to cope with their challenges and find productive ways to live their lives. Some help the homeless find jobs and create new lives for themselves.

Although their focus areas can be very different, the results are always the same: Social workers help people. They learn to do this by pursuing special training in college—either in social work itself or in a subject like psychology or sociology. Once they earn their educational credentials, social workers do their important work in schools, hospitals, government agencies, and private practices.

Go Online to Find Out More!

Find out how the American Red Cross (which employs many social workers) helps people when the worst happens at http:// redcrossyouth.org

SWAT Officer

A Dallas Police SWAT officer rushes to safety with a girl released by an armed man during a standoff. *AP Photo/LM Otero*

Bang! Bang! Bang! Shots keep coming from two masked bank robbers hiding behind the bank tellers' counter. Things didn't go exactly as they planned and they are desperate to avoid getting caught—meaning they are extremely dangerous. Innocent bank employees and customers are being held

What Do You Think?

SWAT members take serious precautions to protect themselves when entering a crime scene. They wear bullet-proof helmets and body armor—often made of an incredibly strong yet lightweight material called Kevlar. What other steps do you suppose they might take in order to be safe instead of sorry?

hostage inside and the situation is quickly going from bad to worse. Who can you call to save the day?

It's the SWAT team to the rescue! SWAT stands for "special weapons and tactics," and SWAT teams are groups of highly trained and heavily armed police officers who are called in when situations get especially dangerous. Situations involving snipers or hostages, people firing weapons in a public place, narcotic raids, and terrorist threats are just a few of the reasons why a SWAT team might be called into action.

Being ready to respond to situations like that at a moment's notice takes a lot of practice and teamwork. Each team member has a specific job to do and they know how to do it. As you might expect, SWAT team mem-

bers generally represent the best and brightest among the department's police force. SWAT officers are experienced police officers with at least a few years of exemplary service to their credit before being selected to train for SWAT. They spend a lot of time training and working through their responses to every possible "what if..." situation they can imagine. They must keep themselves in tip-top shape physically and mentally in order to handle the rigors of this job.

WOW!

SWAT teams sometimes have extra help. K-9 units (highly trained dogs) can be used to find suspects in hiding or to sniff out drugs!

GO FOR IT IF. . .

You're not afraid to stand up to bullies.

- - - - - - - - - - - - - -

You aren't exactly known for being quick on your feet.

FORGET ABOUT IT IF. . .

Even though they are so well trained that if they have to shoot a criminal, chances are very good that they wouldn't miss, SWAT officers would much rather find peaceful resolutions to the tense situations they encounter. Sometimes just the sight of the SWAT team showing up is enough to get some criminals to surrender since it quickly becomes obvious that there won't be a happy ending otherwise. Other times specially trained negotiators can help talk the criminals into giving up. But there are also times when SWAT teams have to do whatever it takes to protect citizens and fellow officers and restore public safety.

Each SWAT team is led by a team commander who is in charge of each situation and must know where all team members are at all times. Yes, that means weekends, holidays, and the middle of the night. Team members must be ready to suit up and go wherever they are needed, whenever dangerous situations occur.

And, yes, being a SWAT officer is as cool as it sounds, which explains why there is a lot of competition for SWAT jobs. But there is also a lot of opportunity too. Every state and most major U.S. cities maintain SWAT teams in their local police departments. In smaller cities, SWAT officers train and respond to emergencies part time while also handling other police force duties. In big cities, though, being a member of the SWAT team is a full-time career move.

Go Online to Find Out More!
Find out more about how SWAT teams work at http://people.howstuffworks.com/swat-team.htm

- -

Teacher

A kindergarten teacher helps a student practice writing the letter *J. Randall Benton/MCT/ Landov*

Look inside a typical American classroom: There sit 30 students (give or take a few). These students may be little kids, big kids, teenagers, or even adults. Whatever their ages, they bring a wide variety of learning styles, learning challenges, and learning abilities. Some speak an entirely different language. Some are dealing with incredibly difficult home situations. Some are bored and looking to liven things up with a bit of outrageous behavior.

What Do You Think?

In what ways do you think schools of the future will be different from the kind of school you attend today? Think about ways that technology might change the way students are taught.

Gutsy Factor

Making the world a smarter place.

Welcome to a teacher's world! Thanks to a teacher's efforts this diverse group of students will ultimately know that Columbus sailed the ocean blue in the year 1492, that the sun is a dying star, and that the United States was once a colony of Great Britain. Before a teacher's work is done, they will know how to think, how to learn, and how to be productive, contributing citizens.

Talk about gutsy jobs! The teachers you encounter at school may not look like heroes to you but they change the lives—and futures—of students every single day. The very fact that you are reading this book is all the proof you need that this is true. Why? Because, chances are, it was a teacher who taught you how to read. Can you imagine how different your life would be now and in the future if you couldn't read or write or do things like adding and subtracting? Thanks to teachers everywhere, kids like you will someday become doctors, authors, or even president! Some of you may even grow up to be teachers too.

Teachers can teach just about anything depending on the school or grade level. Teachers who focus on preschool, kindergarten, and elementary school teach the basics of several subjects; they have to know basic math, science, language, and social studies. At the middle and high school level, teachers tend to only teach one subject, which they become experts in. Some may teach English,

WOW!

The earliest known form of writing developed way back in 3,000 BCE. It was known as cuneiform, and, instead of letters, it used pictures (called pictographs) to represent words and ideas.

GO FOR IT IF...

You're always helping friends with their homework.

Homework? What homework?

FORGET ABOUT IT IF...

while others teach foreign languages like Spanish or German. Still others focus on geometry or algebra or physics. College professors are even more specialized and, in many cases, have earned advanced degrees and gained real world experience related to the subject they teach.

Teachers can get even more specialized in their subjects—some are vocational education teachers, and they help students prepare for careers in health care, business, auto

repair, or technology. Special education teachers help students with disabilities, sometimes using specific computer programs or learning techniques to get the best education for the students. Others teach continuing education for adults to learn new skills.

As you've probably already discovered, there's a big difference between good teachers and bad teachers. The best teachers are totally committed to what they are doing. They love learning, they enjoy working with students, and they are willing to do whatever it takes to make sure that the students who enter their classrooms leave with a better education than they had when they came in.

Go Online to Find Out More!

Have fun with some online learning at http:// funschool.kaboose.com.

More Gutsy Jobs

Facing down wild animals, cutting open peoples' chests to fix their hearts, fighting for democracy in foreign lands—these are just a couple of the gutsy jobs you'll read about here. A word of advice: Scaredy-cats need not apply.

Animal Control Officer

There's a common misconception about animal control officers. Maybe it's from watching too many movies like *Lady and the Tramp,* but some people have the idea that all animal control officers do is ride around and pick up stray dogs, that they are just dog catchers. However, if you've ever had a bat in your attic, a squirrel or raccoon or any other kind of animal stuck in your chimney, or a bear rummaging around your garbage cans, you know the truth—being an animal control officer is a gutsy job.

Sure, there are plenty of stray dogs to pick up, but there are all kinds of situations when animals and people get in each other's way where animal control officers are called in to help. Have you ever seen a dead animal lying on the side of the street one day and then noticed it was gone the next? Where do you suppose that animal went? Chances are pretty good that an animal control officer or two stopped by to scoop up the roadkill. They are also the people who step in and rescue animals when there are situations of animal cruelty or abuse, or in situations where people are in danger because of a wild or diseased animal being somewhere its not supposed to be. It's all in a day's work for an animal control officer!

Cardiac Surgeon

If you asked people to name the most important organ in the body, many are likely to answer, "the heart," although others would think it a toss-up between the heart and the brain! Both are so essential to life that if either one stops working, a person is in big trouble. Which is why the surgeons who keep people's hearts ticking are held in especially high regard.

The work they do is often a matter of life and death and the procedures they regularly perform are risky as well. Common procedures include repairing heart valves inside the heart itself, implanting pacemakers to regulate the heart's beat, performing bypass surgeries to improve blood flow to and from the heart, and, most daring of all—transplanting a heart from one person to another (the donor is already brain dead, of course).

Charity Worker

Charity workers are people who have a passion for helping others who need a leg up in life. Some workers travel around the world to help improve the lives of people in many different ways such as: offering life-saving assistance after a natural disaster strikes; working in refugee camps, taking care of peo-

ple who have been driven from their homelands by war; or helping people in Third World countries become self-sufficient through education and income-producing opportunities.

Other charity-minded individuals work closer to home, providing food and shelter for the homeless, offering care and concern to elderly shut-ins, ministering through a wide variety of faith-based programs, and finding countless other ways to make a difference.

Other types of charity workers organize fund-raising events, big and small, from bake sales at a local school to grand galas involving lots of celebrities and wealthy people. Money raised at these types of events is donated to various charity organizations to help them help others.

Mail Carrier

"Neither snow nor rain nor heat nor gloom of night stays these couriers from the swift completion of their appointed rounds..." So said Greek historian Herodotus about postal couriers delivering mail on horseback during the war between the Greeks and Persians in about 500 BCE. And since 1897, so says the engraving gracing the New York City General Post Office. Although it's not officially the motto of the United States Postal Service, this famous quote certainly describes the dedication of the thousands of mail couriers who routinely brave nature's worst weather to make sure the mail gets through.

And if that doesn't make the job of mail carrier sound gutsy enough for you, consider this: Dogs bite hundreds of mail carriers every year. That doesn't include the thousands of mail carriers who are chased, menaced, and otherwise frightened half out of their wits by out-of-control mutts along their designated mail routes.

If even that doesn't make you tip your hat in honor of mail carriers everywhere, imagine this: According to the United States Postal Services, mail carriers process and deliver more than 212 billion pieces of mail every year—including letters, cards, ads, bills, payments, and packages. Which, in case you were wondering, equals roughly 700 million pieces per day, 29 million pieces per hour, 486,000 pieces

per minute, 8,000 pieces per second. Now that's a lot of mail to get from one place to another!

Military Serviceperson

There are five branches of the military in the United States, and they've each got very specific and important jobs to do in order to protect the country. The Army provides the ground and armored troops who, when duty calls, bravely march into battle, engaging the enemy on the front lines and wherever else they encounter them. Artillery, attack helicopters, and tanks are some of the specialized weapons they use to get the job done.

The Navy patrols international waters in ships and submarines, protecting U.S. interests abroad. They support war efforts using both long-range weapons and missiles to hit targets on land or at sea and by serving as aircraft carriers (or mobile airports) for Navy fighter planes.

Speaking of flying, the Air Force's main job is to protect U.S. interests from the sky, using sophisticated fighter aircraft, tanker aircraft, light and heavy bomber aircraft, transport aircraft, and helicopters. At one time the Air Force's primary wartime role was supporting the Army. In recent conflicts, however, their weapons have proved so dead-on accurate that they are often used to root out the enemy and defuse dangerous situations without endangering the lives of troops on the ground.

Then there are the Marines, considered by many to be the most hardcore of all the military branches. Marines are mostly responsible for "amphibious" assault, which means they come ashore from the water and work their way inland to fight in strategic positions from there. They are also called in when situations call for a rapid response.

Last but not least is the Coast Guard, which uses ships, boats, aircraft, and sea stations to provide law enforcement, boating safety, sea rescue, and illegal immigration control in U.S. waters and territories.

With so many branches to choose from, anybody can become a hero!

Miner

"Miner" makes regular appearances on the world's most dangerous occupations lists—and for good reason. Miners work deep underground extracting valuable minerals and materials from the earth. Miners seek anything from diamonds to salt. Some of the most commonly recovered materials include bauxite, coal, copper, gold, silver, iron, lead, limestone, magnesite, nickel, phosphate, oil shale, tin, uranium, and molybdenum. Generally speaking, any material that can't be grown through natural agricultural processes or manufactured in a laboratory or factory is fair game for mining.

Pits, caves, rocks, quarries, slopes, and shafts are among the places where miners look for these "buried treasures." By all accounts the work is dirty and the worksites unstable. Although employers take precautions to keep things safe (with a little prodding from federal and state laws), there's no getting around the possibility of occasional life-threatening cave-ins or fires.

National Guardsman

After a hard week's work, most people want to kick off their shoes and relax over the weekend. But for members of the National Guard, one weekend a month and two weeks every summer, they have to head to their other job after they leave work on Friday evening.

On those "back-to-work" occasions, they put on military uniforms and become "weekend warriors," reporting to their local National Guard post and preparing themselves to protect their home, state, or country whenever duty calls.

During wartimes or other state or national emergencies, National Guard troops are mobilized and immediately become full-time soldiers (or pilots, or medics, or whatever their particular specialty happens to be). That means they must pack up their bags, tell their bosses they are leaving, kiss their families good-bye, and head out for what may be days, months, or even years of service.

Today Guardsmen are stationed in areas such as Haiti, Bosnia, and even Iraq—serving alongside other military members. They also help protect and save civilians when natural disasters hit, like when Hurricane Katrina smashed into the Gulf Coast in 2005.

Smoke Jumper

There are firefighters and then there are *firefighters*. All firefighters regularly risk life and limb to battle blazes in homes, businesses, and other public places. But there is a special kind of firefighter that takes the element of danger even further. These firefighters are called smoke jumpers. Not only do they battle enormous forest fires, but they often jump out of airplanes near the site of these fires and camp out a bit closer to these raging infernos than most people care to get until they get the fire under control. Now, that takes guts!

Most forest fires happen during the summer months in the western part of the country where hot, dry weather conditions make it possible for even an innocent little campfire left unchecked to ignite a major fire. According to the National Interagency Fire Center, this is not unusual—in 2007 there were 85,705 wildland fires that consumed an estimated 9,328,045 acres of land. Most of these fires eventually burned themselves out. But many of them required the all-out efforts of America's most elite firefighting teams.

Real People, Gutsy Jobs

Here's your chance to get acquainted with four real-life heroes. Their jobs are all gutsy in different ways: One was a top diplomat during a very important point in history, one is a paramedic who rescues people who are hurt or seriously ill, another helps college students think through matters of faith, and another protects citizens from violent criminals.

PEOPLE PROFILE #1: Nguyen Xuan Phong, Ambassador

Ambassador Nguyen Xuan Phong never intended to become one of South Vietnam's most respected diplomats—in fact, the only thing he was planning on was a business career! With the Vietnam War kicking into high gear, though, South Vietnam drafted him to become the Minister of Labor in 1965 when he was only 29 years old.

During the next 10 years, Ambassador Phong got more involved in the diplomatic process surrounding the war. He was right in the middle of official negotiations between South Vietnam, North Vietnam, and the United States. He even led the Saigon (capital of the old South Vietnam) delegation at the Paris Peace Talks of 1968, which attempted to settle the war peacefully.

During the course of his work he met many different ambassadors, delegates, and leaders from around the world, including President Lyndon B. Johnson and South Vietnam's President Park Chung Hee. However, Ambassador Phong would never have been able to talk with all of these people if he hadn't been trilingual—he spoke Vietnamese, French, and English fluently.

His job as ambassador came to an end in April 1975, when Saigon fell and North Vietnam won the war. Ambassador Phong spent the next five years in prison for aiding South Vietnam, but he never forgot the amazing people he met and the wonderful things he experienced. He may not have carried a gun, but he fought for his country with much dedication and courage.

PEOPLE PROFILE #2: Sam Carothers, Campus Chaplain

Seemingly your average college student, Sam Carothers received a call that would change his life and the lives of those around him forever. The call, he says, was from God, and the message was that Carothers should become a minister. After more than 26 years as the campus chaplain at Meredith College, a women's college in Raleigh, North Carolina, he is still glad that he answered.

It may surprise you that it takes a great deal of preparation to be a religious leader. After finishing his undergraduate college degree, Carothers attended a seminary run by his denomination to get his Master of Divinity degree and then took on a yearlong internship, working for a college minister at the University of Tennessee. After all of this, he was ready to embark on the career path he had chosen.

Carothers says his favorite part of his job is seeing students grow, both in their faith and as individuals. His profession has allowed him to impact young people's lives in many ways, as he's seen them study hard and graduate from college, officiated at their weddings, and even worked with *their* children later on when they grew up to attend Meredith College.

It may seem as though college chaplain isn't so gutsy of a career, but Carothers begs to differ. While his position has given him many opportunities to enjoy the students he works with, his job also requires him to deal with students, faculty, and staff when they are hospitalized with critical illnesses and injuries. He must gather up his faith, training, and years of experience to find the right things to say in order to comfort and offer encouragement to the sick and their loved ones.

Hospital visits aren't always sad occasions for Carothers when he's on the job, though: He does get invited regularly to rejoice with the people whose lives he's touched, like when a former student has a baby!

PEOPLE PROFILE #3: Lonnie Knudsen, Paramedic

What would you do if you saw someone who needed immediate medical help? Would you call 911? In a situation like this, phoning for help is exactly what you should do. But what if you could do more?

That's the question Lonnie Knudsen asked himself as he watched a team of paramedics respond to a call he made after he saw a lady take a nasty fall. He was so impressed that he soon began training to become a paramedic.

Being a paramedic takes a lot of guts. Not knowing what is around the corner and working in dangerous environments—scenes with wrecked cars, hazardous materials, and even uncooperative people—means Knudsen has to be on his toes and stay aware of the always-changing situations he's in.

Knudsen's job isn't all flashing lights, wailing sirens, and soaring adrenaline, though. His favorite part of his work is making a positive difference in the lives of the people he helps, even if it's just by greeting patients with a smile or holding their hands to comfort them. He says, "It's an honor when people can put their entire well-being and trust in you to take care of them."

A word of advice from our paramedic: "Being safe is not just something you say, but it's the way you should live life. Be responsible for your actions and how they impact yourself and others. Taking undo risks will surely warrant you an ambulance ride later in life"—something you definitely want to avoid, even if you are rescued by someone as cool as Knudsen!

PEOPLE PROFILE #4: Mike Odle, SWAT Officer

A woman and her child are being held hostage after a shootout in downtown Los Angeles. Across the city a man is standing on the roof of a 12-story building, threatening to leap off. No, this isn't a description for the latest Will Smith action film; it's just a day in the life of Mike Odle, an officer in the Los Angeles Police Department's Special Weapons and Tactics Team (SWAT). He, with fellow SWAT officers, provides citizens protection in situations that cannot be handled by regular police officers.

Odle always wanted to be a cop, but after seeing the LAPD SWAT respond in a highly publicized shoot-out in 1974, he was determined to join their team. The next year he enlisted in the Army, after which he became a member of the LAPD SWAT.

In order to become a SWAT officer with the LAPD, an officer must serve for at least five years, go through an extensive qualification process—including 12 excruciating weeks of SWAT school—followed by six months in a SWAT platoon. After all this, the officer gets a final special rating report, and, if all goes well, he or she is welcomed as a true SWAT member!

The job of a SWAT officer is gutsy—no doubt about that. The gutsiest part according to Odle? Involvement in a hostage rescue, which usually involves extremely dangerous criminals. "Rescue mode," as Odle calls it, is what makes this job both really intense and really worthwhile.

Gutsy Job Playground

You've read about gutsy jobs that other people do. Here's your chance to play around with the idea of having a gutsy job yourself someday. So what do you think? Could you do it? Would you dare? (Oh, and by the way, if this book doesn't belong to you, please use a separate sheet of paper.)

★ Watch Out, Gutsy Job, Here I Come

First, imagine that you're all grown up and ready to tackle a gutsy career...

Would You Do It?	Can't Wait to Try It Someday!	Maybe—If I Ever Get The Nerve!	Not A Chance!
Crash Scene Investigator			
Diplomat			
Environmental Engineer			
First Responder			
Hospice Worker			
Politician			
Religious Leader			
Social Worker			
SWAT Officer			
Teacher			

✪ Mirror, Mirror on the Wall...

Which of these jobs is the most gutsy of them all?

◎ Animal Control Officer

◎ Cardiac Surgeon

◎ Charity Worker

◎ Mail Carrier

◎ Military Serviceperson

◎ Miner

◎ National Guardsman

◎ Smoke Jumper

✪ Help Wanted: Brave Person for a Gutsy Job

Take your pick of the gutsy jobs listed above and pretend that someone's quit the job and you have to find a replacement. Create an ad that will get the bravest, most courageous people racing to your employment office, and make the goof-offs head in the opposite direction! Be sure to weed out the wannabes from the real thing by emphasizing the special talents it takes to get this gutsy job done.

✪ Hot Off the Press!

What's your idea of a totally gutsy job? Can you invent one so challenging and awe-inspiring that people everywhere will be glad to know you are on the job after they read about it?

Pretend that the editor of a weekly news magazine thinks your job is so gutsy that he wants to feature you on the front cover. He asks you to write a short story about what you do. Include a lot of behind-the-scenes information, and don't forget to include some of your most daring deeds!

✪ One More Thing...

Here's some room to list any good books or interesting Web sites you find to further explore gutsy job ideas. You can use a search engine like http://kids.yahoo.com to search for information by typing in the name of a career you'd like to know more about. Or ask your school media specialist or librarian for help in finding some books.

Index

Note: **Bold** page numbers indicate a photo.